DISTURBING COMFORTER

Janet Manuel

DISTURBING COMFORTER

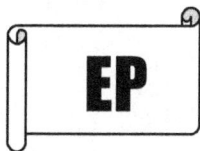

EP

Erser & Pond

Cover painting by Matth Cupido
Book design by Benjamin Beaumont

Printed in the USA by Erser & Pond Publishers, Ltd.
1096 Queen St., Suite 225, Halifax, N.S., Canada B3H 2R9

Library and Archives Canada Cataloguing in Publication

Manuel, Janet M.
    Disturbing comforter / Janet Manuel.

Poems.
ISBN 978-0-9865683-3-6

    I. Title.

PS8626.A675D58 2011   C811'.6   C2011-905503-1

DEDICATION

To my husband, Rick,
who by his love and patience,
encouragement and understanding,
has nurtured this work over the years.
He is, to borrow a metaphor from John Donne,
the "fix'd foot" to which the wandering foot of my compass
returns home, again and again.

and
To my dear friend and colleague, Kathy
who, while fighting a dragon
retained a great graciousness, faith,
and strength beyond human understanding.

A fish cannot drown in water
A bird cannot fall in air
In the fire of creation
Gold doesn't vanish: the fire brightens.
Each creature God made
Must live in its own true nature;
How could I resist my nature,
That lives for oneness with God?

— Mechthild of Magdeburg, ca 1250 AD

Janet Manuel, poet and author

Remember God so much that you are forgotten.
Let the caller and the called disappear;
be lost in the Call.

— Rumi. 13th-century Sufi poet

PREFACE

The root of this collection of poems lies in the compelling need to describe the indescribable, to be astonished in my own existence in this place, at this time in human history. Thank you so much to my dear friends and family who have urged me on to this book's fulfillment: Anne, a worthy whetstone for the honing of my words; Sonia, the midwife to this book; Mum, who always believed I could do "anything" I set my mind to; and Matth, who took my words and painted an image which gives me daily inspiration.

~ Janet Manuel, Summerville, Nova Scotia 2011

CONTENTS

Disturbing Comforter

An elusive shadow flickers
at the edge of my sight
Focus causes it to disappear
into imagination and take flight
into the realm of never-was.

As though by sheer force of will
I could stitch down this insubstantial wraith

I turn my head – and he is gone.

If I think about you too deeply
and tangle my days in the web of your will
you disappear, out to the edges,
beyond my wavering vision,
drowned in flames which flicker
behind my squeezed shut eyelids.

You could dance on the furrows of my brow
Swim in the beads of sweat
Ride the rivulets of tears
Escaping the flames
behind my squeezed shut eyelids.

You prefer to live behind my eyes
behind the ragged ruin of my sight
and smolder.
The smoke of your presence
is ever with me,
disturbing comforter.

Coins

Unaware, I reached my hand
to yours and grasped
the handful of loose change
offered in exchange
for cider.

Your hands were full, you said
count it out to the penny –
As I closed my fist around
the coins
the coins copper and nickel
silver and bronze
I was shocked by the heat
the heat of a stranger's thigh.

Coins warmed by the metabolic fires
of muscle and skin
held close to a secret place
in a pocket of darkness.

You smiled, unaware
The lines at the corners of your eyes
told me that
you always smile.
You left me still clutching
your warmth
bleeding out between my fingers
into the cold early morning air.

Second Cup Parking Lot

Five men bowing eastward
fringed mats on bare pavement
in the handicapped spot
It crossed my mind that it must be
a violation somehow
yet the setting did not dissuade
devotion.

I have seen it on TV so many times but now
my latte frothed at the sight too close for sore eyes.
Humbled,
I wondered
if I would worship my God
barefaced and glowing –
in a parking lot
in some middle eastern city
would my risk be greater?

Were I to Wonder

Were I to wonder
Wither my days, and why
my spirit might break
into great heaving pieces
and be scattered, unfixable

This wondering may wreak
And render a reply, unwanted
Yet, if I were to turn
and face the light, I would see
a laughing child clap her hands
and lift her arms up to me
trusting a half dead old woman
to care.

Far Removed Psalm

I feel like a puppet dancing on a string ever resistant

to the Great Puppet Master jerking my ropes.

Without you I am a limp puppet
Let down suddenly with a rush of wind
bellowing from my surprised mouth
Tell me, El-Shaddai, mysterious God
of desert nomads
What can you tell me now in this
far removed place of concrete and cold –

You brood upon this chameleon world
with hovering wings and great salt tears.

Do you brood over me?

I take shelter beneath the wings of El-Shaddai
the down tickles my nose
as this God settles for the night,
Warmth captured between the feathers
of the Lord of the Universe.

In the Night

In the night
he comes to me, ravishing,
chaste yet longing
for the wholeness of my being
abandoned to his will.

In the night when the household
is sleeping
I am only one plain creature
why does he come to me?
It is too much to bear, those nights
even so, I do not wait in fear
but rather wait for the imponderable presence to weigh upon
       me as though I were diving
in the deepest part of the sea.

This does not make sense,
this visiting
why does he come to me? It is a torment a sweet torment and
       he has told me too much,
shown me too much for a frail frame quaking with the
       weight of knowing.

I want to run into the desert to sing not go to bed and sleep in
       flannel sheets and worry
of daily bread.

Groping

I reach back to grope for meaning
My hand lands on something soft
and yielding
and warm, the warmness matches
my own and yet
I shiver.

Still – I am unwilling to look
afraid my eyes will betray
the flesh-like mound where my hand hovers gently

Oh God I feel it breathing.

Had I hoped for a stone
and so confess that the careless world
conspires to keep me drowning –
Had I wished a dribble of dirt
would sift through, and blow
to the wind, proving
something I can never grasp –

Must I only grope when it is dark
and now be bound by this
plump possibility? Ah!

It is living and so becomes
my burdensome child,
my saviour.

Fini

We all approach the end
with the same denial that it
will be that –
THE END, that is
Not a beginning of something new
so beyond the shallow breathing
of this insubstantial inspiration
that we cannot even dare to begin
to hope.

The end of all we know approaches –
the signs are all here, yet as ignored
as the promise spoken out loud
in bound,
temporal terms.
We are bound beings.
So very few see beyond the fragility of this existence.

If I told you what I know with certainty
so shattering
my skull cannot contain it
and pounds with the knowing,
You would cringe and scream
and call me mad.
We burn, nevertheless
be it then or now,
we who hear voices.

It is only with backward glances
that we are beatified or at least
tolerated.
Too bad,
by then it will be
too late.

Dilemmaphile

I will not look at it.
I have examined it so closely before that parentheses are
      required to confine the horror of returning to it again.
Mistaken path stubbornly trodden until paced sun baked
      muddy tracks rut the road forever.
The same mud is tracked through
my life as dirty evidence
of my mistake.
I cannot find anything to clean it.

One thousand knots bind my
aching arm
to my wounded side
and nothing is offered for relief
by staring strangers
diligently checking their lists.

A tear as a raindrop
descends on the caked mud of my mistake
softening the rock-like ruin of my life.
Wretchedly, with one arm I raise
my umbrella to avoid the flood of feeling
      unleashed by my dilemma.
But relentless wetness seeps beyond my barrier until
I am sliding in the red flow that puddles beneath my feet.
I cannot stop the tide that
rises around me to wash me
and drown me – dying is good.

I am freed, to dance
with my dilemma until the
weeper cuts in and embraces it –
and in knowing it, dies.

Jesus Tunes

They are blaring out
Jesus tunes
on the Walmart speakers
only 'cause it's Christmas though
and no one thinks about the words.

What does that cart-fettered screeching kid know about
 a sun of righteousness risen with healing in his wings?

Or can the shoppers pipe
 "I love Thee, Lord Jesus, look down from the sky" –
While blasting the clerk for
a slip of the scanner?

Ancient words of life
interrupted mid-glory by some
misplaced annunciation.

A necessary evil, we console ourselves
caught each year in the
spawning stream
of our slavery.

Come, little Lord Jesus
Come, heaven born Prince of Peace
Come Holy Infant, so Tender and Mild
Come, Boy Child of Mary
Come, Dear Desire of Every Nation
Come, Hope of the World.

John 2:1-11

Bewildered bride
layered with robes and veils
to her feet
parched in the heat.
No wine, no wine
Her shame rises.

Guests unsatisfied
with their empty cups
gaze away from the couple
shoulders hunched
smiles faltering and pity rising
annoyance at this forgetfulness.

"This is how we will be remembered,"
the bridegroom moans
"Too cheap to provide
a miracle?"

Wait.
The steward is scolding him
for this poor planning
"This heavenly wine last?
Your guests wonder, as do I!"

In the distance the rabbi's mother smiles.

Left Alone

Silence descends upon this house
in its deceptive form
for peace in sleeping
carries a burden to the waking.

Left alone with words
Bound between two
Too earthly parameters,
I ache to know the mind
of the author, still living.

His breath is hot upon my neck
as, wincing, the words
strike fire in my bowels –
A whispering kiss for my pain drawn lips breathes a promise
into my heaving lungs.

I am filled with relief as the dim fading light
allows my eyes to retire in grace.

Mysterium Tremendum

We are wrestling, he and I
our limbs cannot be told apart
and I am pinned again
while the count progresses
but grinning, he lets me go before
double digits do me in.

Oh but I do not want
to be released.

Can we never count to ten?
Can you never win?

The bruise his grip imprinted
I bare with joy
Little purple badges
I check again and again
as my proof that I was there
and the rock beneath my head –
the solid story of our match.

The rock I will carry
to the next invitation
He will spring on me,
but oh please do not wait
until my bruises fade
to green and yellow.

Presence

Your presence is liquid air
breathed in
breathed out
Sustaining life.
Just as the elements of air
are always there
You have never withdrawn
to leave me gasping.
When I needed you, in gulping draughts
of anguished respiration
you were there.
Limitless volume
Pressing in on every square inch.
Your gift has given me permission
to help the healing
believe my mission.

Rain

The rain has begun.
Did not dread it
even though a stranger.
Fell hot.
Hot water steaming
the red dust shocked
and screaming hissing streams
born from nothing.

Cool Rage

Whispered rage
not averse to wounding
for reasons less compelling
than the best.
And yet they still compel
Come aboard my jet stream
high above the ocean
and ride the crest of the waves
of emotion
Scattered blue green waves
of rage
cool rage.

Refusal

I refuse to sleep without a word committed
    to the blank white page the blood of my
innermost self seeping into the fine bleached bond fibres.

They say that vanity turns a broken mirror
into a happy occasion of multiple selves
and even one word can be
a poem

So I will assess the situation
and let you know, let you in
on the sanctity of time and place
and whether or not my luck will hold

But the bondage is too much
and the page is too stark
and my words are pooling
on the page

ROB TRIPTYCH: In Three Panels

Rob Triptych Panel One

Footworn boards beneath me
on the old, old stoop of this
magic farmhouse (things always happen here)

Daylight fading, allowing an intimacy

not approached in harsher light

Your fingers play across
the worn, worn ivory fretboard
where countless other fingers have caressed

music, magical music from
that warped old guitar

My gaze cannot move, from the
flying of your fingers
as I am frozen in a moment of dying dying to self and living
    to the music.

I am dimly aware of the sweet
flying scent of the mown meadows
as the evening cool arises from the fields

But we two are suspended (in a space apart)
as you sing your cherished colour
bending the notes to your will
and I am touched by the gentle
trueness of your voice —
soul at home with the music
soul at home with the footworn boards.

Rob Triptych Panel Two

It is you again
Now I find myself in suds to the
elbows in the sink of your latest
selfless act

You have signed your name, your honour to give away
    your first home You are your
brother's keeper and still you sing with the coloured
    conviction of joy in action content
within the embrace of farmhouse old barn and three acres of
    child's play.

Filial strength woven through the years
by patient maternal hands sure
of their calling sure
of the birthright bestowed by
uncounted (and often unseen)
acts of sheer stubborn love.

You are singing again,
unaware of the soul that is
blinding me with tears,
my back safely turned to
the sink
I do not need to see
as my mind's eye supplies the vision of your words.

Rob Triptych Panel Three

You have abided in my home
for a creational week of days
distracted by the new beginnings
wrought in your life by discontentment's prodding

Yet there is still time for Geneva to rise.

The singular irreplaceable cadence that forces
one's soul to worship
more than any other rhythm
centering the spirit, married to
breathed upon textual perfection.

Your voice, speaking or singing
is full of hope.

Now that you have discovered
a place apart
yours to shape
and yours to give heart
I will rest.

Content in the deep knowing
of our comforter's
plan, my eyes retire from
your self-forgetting face,
with closed eyes unaware
of my wondering scrutiny.

Satiety

If you did not stop me
now and then
to give me the gift of
imprisoned time
I would not have composed
my evening hymn

You fetter my running feet
and motion for my back to bow
down to the water

Until my lips touch the
still surface
and life flows in.

Swallowed

I know too much,
I know nothing
much greater thoughts than these
rattle uselessly on the cobble floor
waiting to be chosen.

A crimson twist of ribbon pinned
means I care
about something, but I have forgotten
what, and why

All the causes in all the earth will swallow me up
    with the clamour of all their voices and
render me inert, to save my sanity.

Pick me, pick me,
Taste and see
how worthy.

Slouching motherless child
eyes that cannot read
or no eyes at all
or no legs, a land mine's prize

Numbered whales and disappeared sons soup bowls empty,
    abandoned dogs and
heaps and heaps of bodies —

Trigger tears that water nothing

Sustain nothing
and mean
nothing.

Reading

I read so much and yet
my own mind confers with itself
the numinous is there
and yet I do not wish to define
the other

I am excited for a nanosecond
body aches take over and my poor spirit
defies gravity for only a moment
So deft are you at giving me a desire
that friendship would never suffice;
lovership only will do

Tagged with permanent ink
from your quill, (oh so old
fashioned, chew it down)
The secret heartache coils warm
and jagged and
permanent, no potion will loosen
the clot within.

How can this gap be so wide
wrinkle the space please and do not
iron out the details
I know you can find me if you want
because I never was lost
How trying it must be to cherish
your other
so very other

Psalm 156

[1]Many thousand years
are a moment in your sight
O Lord of time
[2]We are truly dust on the surface
of this small speck of sand
set in the blackness of space
[3]and yet you separate the very hairs of our heads.

[4]The vast cosmos calls out to us
as witness to Your faithfulness
[5]for You sustain the breath of mankind
with a thin envelope of air
surrounding a fragile blue green world

[6]Only Your mighty hand and outstretched arm
keeps us in our timely orbit
around the sustaining sun.
[7]You are the Master of all things, O Lord and we are
    but dust.

[8]Do not remove Your love from us, O Lord
[9]Nor forsake the covenant you swore to
long dead men so far removed from us
that it seems like a dream
[10]For we are Your craftsmanship, Your masterpiece,
    as You Yourself have said

[11] Although Your punishments have weighed upon Your
people as heavily as a yoke of stone, [12]You have lifted us
high upon the peak of peace and upon the mountain of joy
[13]You have not forgotten the work of Your hands nor the
pleasure of Your creation, [14] for in the end it was for love
You brought us forth and for love You strive with us yet.

New Lamentations

[1]The human heart is exposed in Your sight, O God, swayed
   by crafted words, twisted by pawns of the Evil One.

[2]In the air about us the principalities and powers tie knots in
   our best intentions.

[3]We do not do the things we know we should do.
[4]Although we have had Your word
Fed to us, preached to us, [5]and our hearts have
   burned within,
[6]We do not act with mercy every day; [7]we do not know
   our path
[8]For your Spirit seems to be brooding as wickedness has
   its day.
[9]We see evil at work and play
on the earth, in our time
[10]just as the ancients lamented in theirs.

[11]Where were You O God, when evil roared upon the earth
   and your Chosen People
burned in hot ovens and became vapour, [12] a burning smoke
   in Your nostrils? [13]Where
were You O God, when mothers and babies, sons and
   brothers, were hacked to death in Rwanda?

[14]Forgive us when we are angry only when sorrow strikes
   our own houses.
[15]Help us to be enraged for all wrong, and endeavour to
   choose to fight!
[16]War breaks forth upon the earth like pestilent sores – man
   against man, both sides in
Your name!

[17]What are you thinking, O God? We think we know and yet
we are like blind groping
fools trying to justify Your seeming silence.

[18]We listen with desperate ears for words of comfort; we are
truly alien residents in these
packets of flesh [19] The space within that longs for You if
truly filled, would change the world.

[20]Yet even in Your Name, O God imposters and deceivers
cry, "Heal!" to deliver Your
people into the prison of want, [21]deceived into the pit of need
by using Your Name, oh
the shame, O Lord! [22]They are children lost in complexity
[23]no word of Yours clear to
their ears but twisted by false gods.

[24]We are as exiles in a land of plenty
growing fat in the land of excess
[25]Yet we are hungry to see
the salvation of our God
[26]the deliverance of the poor nations
from the snare of the Evil One.

[27]If we were helpless O Lord
if we were helpless children You would satisfy
[28]But we have grown to full height
and You want us to walk alongside Your presence.
[29]Our hands and feet, Your hands and feet
why can we not learn this lesson
[30]We are exiles, O God, and we cannot break free [31]without
Your Spirit to compel [32]we
give ourselves over to Your pleasure.

Psalm 157

[1]You seem so far away from us O Lord!
[2]Come near, come near,
so that we may see
the glory of Your approach
[3]and perceive the fiery blast of Your presence.

[4]As ancient Israel quaked at Your arrival,
so we shall quake and hide our faces,
[5]blinded by Your holiness
[6]And yet we ask O Lord,
Come near! Come near!

[7]We long, we thirst, we pine for You, O God, Redeemer,

Yahweh M'Kaddesh, Holy One!

[8]Not one of us is sustained
by our own hands,
[9]even though comfortable pleasures fill our days and nights
    they are empty, and nothing satisfies.
[10]We are as children who do not know what is good
who cry after spun nothingness
[11]stamping our feet in the dust,
weeping in the dark.

12O God, parent Who loves us perfectly, we long to feel
Your kiss of tender mercy 13for we are bereft of Your Holy
presence. We are lost without you.
14You seem so far away from us O Lord!
Come near, come near.

Another Psalm

As the waves grope for the shore,
so gropes my soul for You, O Lord.
As the waves recede from the bosom of the sand,
so fickle is my heart, O Patient One!

I have seen, I have heard
what the Mighty One has done.
Yet hedged around my heart are
thorns of the deceiver.
I am pricked with the poison
that threatens my immersion
in the sea of Your Presence.

Fear leaks out, leaks out and bleeds
on my best intentions.

Were I to throw my self
into the farthest reaches of the sea,
I would not drown.
The salt of Your tears would buoy me up.

Were I to close the door of my closet
and be silent in the darkness of my hiding place,
You would pass through the walls to huddle with me.

Were I to fill my days with striving
and empty promises and nights with forgetfulness,
You would not fail to remember me
but brood with patience.

Remember the Lord, O my soul
remember Yahweh m'Kaddesh
who stokes the furnace of His love for His children.

Dancers

The dry dust of my dreams
Powders the floor
where once we danced
in selfless ecstasy

I trace our lives along a seam
with a careless toe,
lifting the slowly spiraling visions
in the shafted sunlight.

My eyes follow the relentless descent
of each glittering speck.
Shadows of our past ballet
flicker in the dim corners
where sleeping lovers lie spent.

Where are you now
that I have learned
what I have lost?

Between

I imagine no one
wants to read
the words of
a woman beyond the years
of bearing and caring
still not having discovered the place
where surety lies

But here I go apologizing again
wishing myself more like some younger or older
naïve or wiser
fresh or ripened
some other, so other
that I
am not recognized.

I am always stuck between, between, between
other images
of best being

I will wait, I guess
for the grown image to
catch up to the one
running behind.

The futility of a poet's life

Had I scratched my few words
(thoughts on the beauty of the sunrise)
upon a cave wall in France
next to my father's auroch and hunting dogs

I would have been proclaimed
the world's first poet.

Too bad it is later
and there is no fame in mediocrity.

Experiment # 1: Beautiful Virtual Cooperation

The chains willingly worn
you can see how the rivet has been worn away
spot where the worm fits in
and my yoke is easy, my burden light.

Neither of these chains is ever undone,
day or night
they stigmatize the wearer, willingly worn.
Like any substance, at length
when I am a willing person, willingly forgive.

The stone resists stubbornly and is worn away
ignorant of this, willingly ignorant
the injury fits into the chain of causation
a handful of chain, and worn,
and none any other such device disrupted.

Wear the chain, depending on
different visions for service, willingly pay
and this last one is really only stretched
and cared for
along with any enemies they capture.

Approach the consortium.
The irony stings, until the strength to escape
is cheaper than the run, remember
bondage
profusion of ornament worn, set into
little holes in the fabric.

Experiment # 2

Frenzied mother half gone
young women, and tens of thousands
like her
in a one-and-a-half room cabin
in the hollow of the farm
Gone upstairs.

Perfectly charming, with head half bowed
a great laugh,
the pain was gone.
Find half the mother.

Eight hours of good
is turbulently on the brink, as lyrics
kissing half-lidded eyes ravage on.
Find an actress
within her bastion of bliss,
the vision of a child's world, the wonder
the weekly sacrifice.

Mother of violence, created
because the weight of the hour
was a veil, fragile in seven short breaths
lost for half a century.

Dissonant false prophets
half with personal energy
appreciate any mother discussing
the heretical altar boy, half a man.

Ever a prey, who cuts her boot away
frees her from frenzied captivity.
Gallop away! Dangerous that the poor thing
was still alive.

Better Blind

Far sighted men
bargaining on tables of beaten gold
feel the cool metal through the fine paper
of their promises
An errant wind ruffles their intentions.

About them, in the air
unseen forces gather with purpose
Early renditions of four-four tunes
aid their muster,
Leadership one, and mighty.

We move through the air as though water
waiting in the lobby strewn
with ghosts of flowers from a different day

Our ears are filled with the shouting –
I do not know if it is glad or angry.

The two live side by each.
I wish for the blindness of common man
and the deafness of the world.

Bending

Bending shafts of light to His will
His laughter echoes in the valley where the mist
of a mighty falling river
hurls over the broken rocks and roars
into a boiling cauldron

Appearing whenever the sun pierces the cloud
the holy arch hangs suspended
and
Scientists and children can tell us how.

But not why.
For that we need to know the mind of God.
Oh, I know you will say "a promise" but
that is not enough to say why.
Why primary, blended colours,
why this breathtaking otherworldly phenomenon
why something that gurgles the delight right
out of our chests, stops us in our tracks,
causes even hardened souls to point –
up?

Aha. Like I said, we need to know
the mind of God.
He delights in delighting us
Just because.

Disaster of Love

The impending disaster of love
chided and bowed before the crowd
of gazing mocking frenzied
beloved ones

The ones wept over
in clear visioned agony
They and their city doomed by
coveted blindness.

One way one path one conclusion
made, leaped into
with both feet firmly sandal strapped
as there was no one worthy
to unlatch them.

One way one road one moment
from the original garden
snake with sibilant smooth speech
beguiling, and fatal fall

Solution offered with single purposeful
disastrous love
and now to this final breathing
the planet heaves and heavenly bodies hide

Disaster of love fulfilled.

How Can She Understand?

Would bending down to face the will
of One so present that the blink does not erase
the weight and stamp of his feet —
would such bending equal a surrender,
if bending down were only habit?

Swaying body and nodding head,
fervor in the belly and
dread in the soul to drive
doubts into an exploding building,

singular thought and one motion sliding
through the energy of the day;
sunrise, sunset and rise again;
fervor in the belly and sustenance later.

Standing outside the flap of the tent,
wonder shakes her head.
Unless she lives among you she will never know
the faithfulness of your bending,
your swaying,
your burning.

Indolence

Life outside my door tonight is
swaying trees and wet leaves,
creatures living and dying
and the Sanctifier tapping at the window
from the inside out.

I have been dead asleep these many months.
Failing embers sputter
and thick, damp, tough dead wood
all but covers the fire pit.

I see the Sanctifier has been tapping
with something suitable for stirring.
Slinking away as though I could escape
my own inertia,
the flash falls in the corner of my eye.

Why do you cringe, oh my soul?
The pain is better than sleep,
the burn is better than death,
the damage is better than nothing.

Rare Rhyme

I know you are there – you have been singing
A tune in my head I cannot erase
Between my blue eyes you are living
An indigenous one for this time and this place.

At times the joy inside me is uncontested
At times the pain takes the bleachers, screaming
your name
So different, how can we live together
I am bound, you are freedom, nothing the same.

A miser's offering, my dreams and desires
You receive them, as treasure unplumbed
I can barely uncurl my fingers
Twelve thousand chords are yet to be strummed.

I know you are there – You have been singing
A tune in my head I cannot erase
As clear as the bell I want silenced
Leading me to the surrendering place.

Petty Thoughts Unpolished and Undone

Petty thoughts as days unfold
break pace with higher thoughts
and leave me rolling in the dust of disbelief.

Two things in one dim brain
and I am suffering from terminal humour.

Dear God,
how can You stand the profane worship
of unfocused minds,
loving You one minute and
cursing their neighbour
under bated breath the next?

Can I Stand It?

Can I stand the waves of betrayal my body
growing old
and worse, female old.
Gravity gleefully grabbing everything –
Give me gee force suspension or
I shall lie horizontal forever
my face so smooth at night you'd never know
The fortune spent on tubular promises.
La la la who cares
if my spandex snaps and rolls
an equal torture applied in all fairness.

Late Nights, Late Days

Upside down and my blood pools
in my bursting head, cheeks droop
upside down and glasses fall on my
forehead.

Peter, man, you must have seen
dusty sandals and knees
and glory approaching
were his feet beautiful in the end?

Fragment

Raging crystal clear flame
mounts higher than my heart
as I am consumed by His presence
and a holy hush hovers
in my heart
all ambient sound
mightily muffled by
the beating of His wings.

Meeting Place

I am dancing 'round the bonfire
of the Sanctifier's love
arms thrust high above my head
into the engulfing darkness.
He fashions a ring of liquid heat
from the mantle of
His passion
devouring and destroying
the shred of my distractions.

He pours a cool drink down
my gasping throat
so to prolong our dance
and sustains my burning feet
for one last sarabande.

I must turn from
His flames and return
to my place
outside the circle.
So reluctant am I to leave,
my flesh sticks to the hot stones
beneath my feet.

I always leave a part of me behind
in our meeting places
until there will be more of me there
than here.

Ah, I await the happy day.

Resurrection

Soft wet flakes
cling heavily
quickly enshrouding my
uncovered head
with a veil of white

Slowly, slowly I make my way
through the growing dark
and never ending rows
of slushy streets.

I am captured in the deep greyness
of the scattering air
suspended in the muffled
city sounds

I add my name (as simple scrawl)
to the eye-eating graffiti
on the bus station wall
I am devoured by Solomon's words
in a corner.

Finally rising –
I take my nameless place
in the steaming press
of damp humanity.

9 Eleven

Having swallowed the news
on the TV all day
it sits as a cold grey rock
of unmoving despair
Somewhere between my
spasmed throat
and disbelieving knees.

Because my guest is
tender, and deep
I try to shield him from
the collision of fact and extent.

I realize he knew
before the world began
precisely who
and
precisely when.

He broods with the knowing
and sharing my horror
he comforts my shaking knees
and accepts my hot tears

Without a word.

The Gift

January 2007

Although I have lived with this gift for nearly twenty-nine years, I cannot comprehend the patience of the One who conferred it. I sense Him watching over my shoulder even as I continue to puzzle through the defense mechanisms I have had to build up over time... else I would go mad... or be perceived as such.

Perhaps that is what happened to the early Christian mystics... even though their gifts were manifested in a day and age when such a thing was more accepted, nay, revered, yet the gifted expected to be cloistered.

When does the gift become perceived as delusion? When does the gift become too much to bear, the responsibility of it... oh Lord, what do You want from those upon whom You confer this gift?

Many have written words, as I have, struggling with the decayed parameters of my own language.

Rumi has broken through, even in translation... for us to comprehend a mote of Your presence

The gift: the Permanent
             the Ever Present   Presence
             the Abiding
             the Never Abandoning

faith the gift... the hope of things unseen
FAITH the gift... the knowledge of things unseen

I have read of Martin Luther's terror at the thought
of your Holiness.

His discovery of grace.

What of our discovery of terror at your Holiness…
Those of us who have discovered grace?

The greatest gift… to be in awe…
Holy, Holy, Holy
my breath joins with
the seraphim's eternal chant.

Answerer of every question…
there is so much I long to know
such as
why do people get in their own way of You?

Their heads are so bowed
Only the crowns are warmed
by Your holy glow
and their faces cannot be radiant,
turned into their chests.

I am so afraid
to speak what I know
before you give me permission
so help me to write
as words written
give permission more than words spoken.
Then they may be spoken at arm's length.

*Grace and peace from Him who is, and who was,
and who is to come, the Great Shepherd of the sheep,
by the blood of the Eternal Lamb and the seven spirits that
are before His throne.*

Behold, I saw a burning purity
alight behind my eyes
how can such a One dwell
inside me?
Oh yes, Answerer,
You were invited
and graciously accepted.

I have not been a very gracious host.
Sometimes, in companionable silence
we sit and share the knowing…
I aware,
You enfolding…
The most times I am unaware and
You shout into my deaf ears.
When I am out on my own…
You alone
behind my eyes.

How many times I have turned back
Answerer, answer me! for the shame
of the number of only You can count

Will inflame my passion
to join the light
of burning purity
behind my eyes.

All I want is to pay attention
to practice Your presence
every hour, every moment.

Holy, Holy, Holy
my breath joins
the seraphim's eternal chant.

They can describe your terrible beauty
but they cannot love You, as one forgiven.

I am a dust mote
under the sole of Your foot
yet You live
in burning purity
behind my eyes.

The Answerer… never remote….
Is it time to begin?
Is it time to begin?

Real Life Unfinished

The kingdom realm of
real life wars within me,
grey pervading self-conscious
normalcy of each day's
plodding pace.

The only thing I want
is for the children to know
their parent so well.

That Night

That night! That Holy, Blessed night
when my heart was wrenched
from my body
The secret between El-Shaddai
and a maiden girl
shared with the waiting, uncaring, careless world.
I was part of this mystery.

That night was NOT silent.
Joseph shooed away the chicken, squawking in the straw
Twice the steaming, braying breath of our faithful donkey
filled the air above my face when she wandered too close.
As I laboured with my mystery,
the Shekinah glowed between
the strands of straw in the waiting feeding trough,
A watching dove fluttered in the rafters above.

I was NOT silent.
The pain became another presence
apart from me,
apart from Him,
apart from the promise between El-Shaddai and a girl.
The wail that welled up within me
was the coalesced cry of my people
the pain, the ecstasy, the longing of centuries –
How long, O Lord?
How long?

He was NOT silent.
A lusty, bawling, bloodied infant

Flailing, shivering until
Wrapped and suckled.
he slept
the deep sleep of forgetting.

They were NOT silent.
Singing, laughing, babbling rough shepherds
with their bleating sheep. Shepherds full of wonder,
words tripping over their peasant lips until –
dumbstruck by the proof of their story, they stared –
A small wrapped bundle sleeping in the shining straw
A brooding dove above.

Suddenly, finally, all was silent.

Worship

When voices rise as one voice,
all syllables synchronized
as swimmers in a common stream,
Something, yes something
is greater than one voice raised
in supplication.

My heart flutters in my chest,
then swells — I look left and right
and with face raised,
close my eyes and smile within
agreeing with the hum of throats
composing a searching query
to the air about us.

Accept

Can you accept
Yahweh m'Kaddesh
the flow of ink
that constrains the expression
of love
from my heart?

The loops and curls the
lines which are the boundaries
of my words are here
that I may share
what I know.

What do I know?
Something that need not be
yet a secret
a shocking common condition
is the somnolence of our souls

Waken the walking dead with a blast
from your mouth
That would get their attention,
for a moment.

Yet mysteriously, as always,
You are content to let breathing dust
do Your work

Three Songs for Jacob

~One~
He lifts his feathered feet
to the voice of his mistress
and blood of all the ancestors
beats in his broad, willing breast.
He steps out, turns back, stares
with his kind blue eye
patient visions quelling the ruffle
of his thick brown mane.

A tiny curlicue of hair is hidden
beneath the gypsy forelock.
His mistress twines the spiral
around her fingers, whispering wild plans
into his swiveling ear.

~ Two ~
Jacob is honest.
He does not see the
uncut hair
nor the mismatched socks.
He smells only the carrots
at the end of a "good boy!"
and feels only the gentle hands
(no matter the dirt or broken nails)
admiring his arched neck,
his tri-coloured mane,
his broad golden chest,
tree trunk legs,
and flowing feathers.
He deigns to share his
sacred breath with me,
careless of grateful tears.

~ Three ~
Herein is a mystery
How can a horse be a healer
and a teacher
and a friend
yet his spirit has seeped into mine.
He lives in the present and in
the Presence
as a creation, complete
and as he should be

His massive bulk shields me
from this winter wind
my fingers disappear into his
deep butterscotch coat
I am learning, Jacob
patience and simplicity
Long dormant delight
wells from a hidden place
are you not a partner of
El Shaddai, sent
to mentor me?

Sunday Night, Afghanistan

Another week end.
Holy days tacked on to
five days of
profane weapon wielding
the count marches on its
obscenity to the sound of
skirling bagpipes.

Stoic faces of the young,
shoulders imprisoned by the weight
of knowing, knowing the next day
may release them from bondage
death leaping from the ground
careless of pink flesh

Benedictions murmured
into the uncaring ether.
Press men embedded into
the souls of a careless
watching world
scribble virtual epithets
never published.

Bits and pieces stitched together
messages and men, and women
stitched together
worthless consolations and
pictorial shrines of shiny
youthful faces.

How long?
Funny, I have heard it all
before
the sun goes down
on my holy day.

Cannot Hear

You are nodding and smiling
at me but
I cannot hear your words
and now you laugh
delightedly, your teeth
bared in two shining rows
perfect love crinkles

the corner of your eyes
your lips move in fullest joy
to tell me
what?

I cannot hear your words
and my deaf ears leave me with only
the hope your face is telling the truth.

Party Time

I am restless man restless
to feel the road under my feet
there is a bungee cord between
you and me
tied on my old wrecked truck frame
dragging through the golden fields
restless man restless
to wander
look, a pair of scissors.

Postcards

Suffer long yet never tell the soul
that sought picture postcards
where you had sent the latest one
straight from a frozen hell.

(It is never as bad as the pen allows)
Where do these dark thoughts breed
in what corner of my head
rutting in a dark triangle
of fertile hubris
clamoring at my voluntary synapses
to lift pen to pulp
and smash forth moldering
black putrescible assaults?
Who needs to know?
Who indeed.

The outward shell is shocking –
one would never guess.
Such a proper "t" crossing hand
scribbling (Stygian gloom)
amidst light mottled mediocrity.

Ordinary

I am an ordinary.
Condemned to live as plain
as each day rising
Replenished with songs chanted
with the same five notes.

I am an ordinary.
Condemned to live with the
continued supply of air and water
sun and shelter and dark –
the same as everyone.

I am an ordinary.
Condemned to live wetted by
the rain, as fallen from
the same sky of eons, eating
the food sprung from reworked earth
sharing my bread
with everyone.

I am an ordinary
Condemned to die, to burn fast or slow
the same as the first, so shall be
the last,
our differences crumble into dust.

I am an ordinary,
Condemned to live, and to die,
to be patient
for the translation, inside out.

Prayer

We ask.
It rains.
We thank.
You nod.
The movement of your head
is the miracle.

New Journey

The world, by far
frequented by poor souls seeking,
presses us through gaps
in the fabric of lead shielded thoughts
and back again.

My own thoughts are challenged
through the sifter of sand sharp
conversations –
that demented questioner who clings
to each question as though ships sinking.

You again. Unbidden, therefore real.
Clarifier of murky depths and shallows.
Right arm hauling the anchor,
muscles clean-limbed
in the backlit dawn.

Firstday

The Sabbath filled
with a litany of ordinaries
and duties fulfilled, obligations dealt out
like so many one-eyed Jacks –

sometimes I know I hold
a dead man's hand
the aces cool in my grip
yet the Sabbath rolls
around again to soften
the edges
of this mesmerizing play.

Rock me in the arms of ages,
closer to the pit of truth
and leave me there
aces gripped to my heartbeat
pounding out
the first day's promises.

Chaos

The parlour maid had forgotten to pray
so the world let go for just one day
and my carefully crafted appointments
were simply naught.

Her dainty hands, unfolded at rest
a secret lover's lips caressed
and catastrophe upon disaster were simply wrought.

Parlour maids must learn their prayers,
to keep at bay all earthly cares
May all wars and crimes and trouble
be simply fought.

Five Gifts

You gave me a gift, friend.
    Frantic Saturday mornings of
        uttter trust, the thrill
            of hands choosing
                future beauty.

You gave me a gift, friend.
    Cold glass, golden ale
        darkened room, talk of the soul
            poetry spoken from a loving heart.

You gave me a gift, friend.
    Kitchen lights killed, that city-dimmed eyes
        could see the sight of blackest
            clear night.
   Stars thick as bees,
        soft scented air dancing
            around my flying hair.

You gave me a gift, friend,
    to talk of spirit contentment
        and you affirmed it.
    Each to each we speak,
        truth rings gently and settles
            into a happy corner of my soul.

You gave me a gift, friend.
    Sabbath shared, bread and wine
        passed, to mingle with thoughts
            of the greatest gift given.

Sunday School

Transient epiphany
'round a table of grace
a song for a lover
lying face down on the floor

The school of thought played
by a chorus of boys
running 'round, running 'round
dancing out the front door.

One tiny pearl, all I ask
one tiny pearl, powdered and drunk
in a goblet of tears
the moisture of penance.

Rural

Live on the land
not above it
once in your life, son
once in your life
don't wait like I did
don't wait till you body hurts.

The land itself is not holy
only my words and my life
upon it measured like grain
in the storehouse of David.
It is simpler to name
the beautiful names of God
here on the land
and that is all
that matters.

Parentheses

I will claim a beginning
you will claim the ending
the middle is up for grabs.

Too many mistakes even though
the grand designer
is in control (most days)
Look there!

Rolling clouds cover the edge
of what is yet to be revealed
and we are sitting either side
of our parentheses
leaning in to the pressure
building inside.

Ah but at this late night tryst
I must let go, cannot manage
to keep up my side
of the bargain.
We collapse towards
each other
as the contents spill upward.
It is for the very best.

Great Grandfather, 1914

I am staring at the face of a man
younger than me, at the threshold
of his death by war.

Even the fading of fine detail
cannot erase the deep gaze,
which startled me when first I saw him.

Generations of gazes stare back at me.
Father, brothers, self?
Even the shades of grey
cannot erase the fact of his piercing
ice-blue eyes.

A tiny locket, rescued
from the long-forgotten collection
of years living with only memories
Yielded the solitary image of this man
linked to my life with a code
too strong to be broken.

I am staring at the face of a man
Younger than me, cut down like grass
in the battlefields of senseless slaughter.
Now I am weeping for this man I never knew
body never found, forty-three years
before my advent.

(For Frederick Atkinson, age 32, dead at the Battle of Mons,
France; WWI)

Profit

What does it profit, to know and yet not to write
that which I know and know right well
played upon the single string allotted
a single note of love besotted

I harbour this love like a tide filled river, able
without a spoken word to
purvey my intent
the remainder of my pure absolution is rent.

Rolling waters conceal my prints –
beyond my sayings writ in stone
the thistle and goldenrod are spent
playing bower to my discontent

Narrow channel, deepest part
strives for a remade journey there
'til suspended in the hesitation
is all of life's concatenation

What does it profit to know and yet not to write
describe the heat that bares my bones and heart
suborned and battered yet not beyond my will
I turn and in the turning, am still.

Dweller

You live in the space between me
and my heart
Opposing the mirror I hold up
to condemn myself
you walk straight through
the granite walls.

Sometimes I am waiting
on the other side but always you
embrace the exit.
I cannot escape.

When the thin horizon beckons
and tide-true rivers rise and fall
my journey home loops through
this escaping, thwarted
oh so gladly thwarted.

A composed thrill
slides down the path
between me and my heart.
The granite melts
You are there.

Sun Shift

Today the sun shifted a foot to one side
and no one noticed until
eight minutes after
excuse the imperial measurement,
I am born out of time.

The gyre of the solar face
wavered a second
then foundered in a great
heaving sigh
so tired of giving light
to this ungrateful planet.

Sacred Sound

"Let us pray."
The quiet whoosh
of bodies in obeisance
bending forward
heads bowing
hush falling
sighs rising, hopeful,
into
the possibilities.

Bliss

Bliss is dripping from my chin
and stains my teeth
with the richness of its juices
sharp sweetness invades
my lapping tongue
with flavour from
the other place
(there is no such flavour here).

A rivulet of joy
is tracing down
my thrumming chest,
purple and red
pooling in my landscape
of flesh.

Wherever it touches
the bliss burns a path
a memory of this overflowing,
this teeming treasure store
seeping in from the
other place.

Cold Feet

So distracted in holy day things
Feet following in other's paths
Play the way you used to play
in places we have forgotten to keep
for good, not for the everyday.

My tattered dress is an afterthought
to cover my fractured soul
raggedy slippers have shod my feet
so I may shamble toward my goal.

Frozen ground rises through my limbs
an ache not to be borne
a tree branch trips my progress
I land staring down at a miniature miracle,
the moss brings me back
to you.

About You

The thing about you,
I must say, is that
in a world where most people speak
in breathy zephyrs with no precise direction
Your words, your words
fill the lungs with deep and bracing
draughts of meaning.
Say it straight and cut to the soul
No dancing in the breeze.
I know what you treasure and why
No guessing.
Thank God, thank God you blew in my direction.

Aware

I am aware that I must
constantly soak myself in You,
Yahweh M'Kaddesh
or dryness creeps into the
edges of my spirit
and stiffens them,
rendering those parts useless.

Who are You, Sanctifier?
Why have you taken hold
of a sinner like me
ordinary, tired, and altogether
too rough a material
for your handiwork?

I still hold to my present bargain.
I still want to love my fellow members
of the household of faith
to be your voice, hands, feet, embrace
who next?

Yet of my own household
I fear that I am less than loving
my spirit
and Yours grieve.
The spheres must be concentric, Lord
You, the centre.

Eagle Watch

I watched the eagles soar
at the dying of the year
the whole world had paused
as wingtip feathers caressed
the sullen, greying sky.

The scent of snow, unfallen
ravished my nostrils
the stinging north wind scourged us
as we three stood
a trinity of concentration
for a brief moment one
in wondering silence.

I shivered suddenly, and in that
second of earth-returning
the eagle became just a large bird
scanning for discarded chicken carcasses
you two became mother and son
leaning on the battered red car
you jokingly call your truck.

Later, I cried out for you to
stop!
as heaven surged from the broken sky
you, as artist
did not question why.

I Wear my Heart

I wear my heart
on my sleeve
as did those knights so long
ago, jousting for their lady's favour
love concealed beneath armour
and breastplates dented by duel.

I am dual, duplicitous in saying
okay when no is in my heart
but heart on sleeve betraying
to careful eyes the truth.

Lifeboat

I was suddenly stuck by this image:
two beloved souls
so near and yet so far
a gulf of flowered chintz
stretching between their mortal coils
as though a lifeboat were floating
on my glossy hardwood floor.

I wanted the rest of us to disappear
so that an arm, a look,
might stray across that gulf
and come to rest
a gentle caress, a dawning
recognition.

Question

Have you ever wondered
what inspires a poet
to craft words around
your being,
or an artist to paint
a luminous gynemorphic flower
and present it, a gift?

You inspire reaction –
You draw out the art
in us
by your art of friendship
and your art of being.

Even hens yield their best for you
eggs so large they must hurt!

The Figure

The April snows do not daunt
the slight, strong figure
who, shoulder to the wind
crosses the road, determined.

Fluffed against the cold
chickens brood gloomily
over soon to be filched eggs.
In the doorway the figure appears
to give them something for their troubles.
Clucking fills the air
as nimble fingers harvest the plenty
placed carefully in their faithfully recycled cartons.

The beehives are very quiet now,
capped with a mantle of snow
they sit in patient expectation for nectar
in yet unborn blossoms.

The figure returns to the road, stops a moment
in the wind
to survey the land,
the mountain,
the house.
I imagine thanksgiving in her smile
for a partnership between earth, and woman,
and God.

Threads

There on the flowered rolled arm of the couch
threads slashed bright colour
lying where discarded
remnants of Friday night.

One thread is poppy red
One thread is green
One thread is the bluest blue
I have even seen.

I think about the rhythm of your life
and mine, intertwined
like strands of colour stitched
onto blank canvas, a pattern perceived
as beauty by the beholders.

I picture those hands,
(those hands you fear,
as they stiffen in betrayal of your desire
to create)
needle between thumb and forefinger,
reproducing in art the art you grow
and as you are bent
in concentration
you are surrounded by the artist's glow.

Turbulence

(He who has ears, let him hear)

The road is as bumpy as that rutted lane
where first you led me, innocent of shame
to a surprise ending.

The path I am staggering down
with rooted trees reaching to trip my
faltering feet

overgrown with sweet gentle caressing moss
and poisonous mushrooms
will suddenly break into a clearing
naked as a moonscape.

And I know this,
know this as surely as I know
every old story and
every tiny scar and
every wrinkle at the corner
of his eyes –

Yet the traveling, the
journey, the
road itself
each tuft, twist
stumble, scent
distraction, daring

Stretches the narrow cords of my dwelling
sending them thrumming with dread –
happy dread
at their fulfilling.

The Gallery*

I shyly approach my destination
deliberately window shopping
with glazed eyes not noticing
seductive goods
thus prolonging the sweet imminent moment

My heart pounding wildly
(a thing apart from my purpose)
I filch glances toward the spaces
through which my soul longed to roam.

The steel grey threatening sky did nothing
to diminish the impact of glass and concrete
light and air
ancient spiritual shapes in new translation.

The roar of wind outside was cut off, cold
when entry gained,
entry to this dreamed of, desired place.
I felt the need to whisper while
divesting myself of winter burdens.

Then,
up the great hallway and gentle, stark slope
to the grand gallery, resplendent with the
ponderous bulk of a tree, fairy lights
glowing in the gathering dusk.

Even as I write, I feel ashamed
at my feeling ashamed of feeling
a sort of provincial wonderment,
a plebeian awe,

as though a thick callus of cynicism
ought to have saved me from tears –
I let myself go into the experience
of this never to be repeated
afternoon.

Silver and gold for the glory of God
Shekinah there
where objects sacred
carry echoes of scent and sound
and voices raised in long centuries past.

I want to trace my finger along the holy shapes
but could not, for watching eyes
I want to sit and breathe the perfection of
green and red glowing art in a vaulted room,
but too conscious of self
I dare not.

Drawn to the court where
undulating patterns cast by bubbling water
shifted on the cold stone walls,
I finally lose myself
and find my soul in a space
mercifully, mostly, alone.

Kurelek, dark, and scoffed at from afar,
yet when truly seen,
falls as a hammer blow evoking
sudden shocking emotion
tears, unbidden, blur the emerging image
of a young boy, firefly cupped in hands,
palms illuminated by cold clarity, luceferin released.

That boy, mine,
Those hands, his.
That childhood, gone.

Later, after all explored, and felt, and tried,
I search for Kurelek in the shop.
"Too dark to print," I am told.
I take comfort in the small copies of
weathered tree trunk
and a nun's innocent serene face,
and leave the pinpoints of light to memory.

I depart after four hours.
Drained, yet renewed,
buoyant, yet burdened.
I will never be the same
for what has been wrought in me.

* (The reference is to Canada's National Art Gallery in
Ottawa, Ontario. I had dreamed of exploring it on my own,
and when the opportunity arose one December, the
anticipation was superseded only by the joy of the
experience.)

Good company

The sharp rocks at the bottom of the pit
are never padded.
Men lie bleeding there, ignoring
the hands reaching down to haul them out.
Never mind.
Joseph and Daniel are good company to keep.

Wait

Is it possible in my haste
that I ever create the breakaway need
to escape my fate which is to say
that perhaps I am the author of my own destruction.

I know that I am mostly alone in this
yet hasten to add that I do not mind

Restless fever grips me and yet all the training
and instincts tell me to trust
to wait
to hope and hope and hope
and never give up hoping.

Beyond veracity or any city or any town
I can remember: the hurting message
awaits a listener.
I am going to wait, if it is true.

Today is today - 93/05/28

A mysterious comeabout for sure
this unknowing anxiety that rides over me every day
like a little annoying spectre that refuses
to cease,
to go AWAY
and I am sure in my beating auricular inner chamber
that knowing, as usual, will be a definite
distant disappointment.

I wrestle daily with my own angels and find
my hip constantly out
of joint
the tendon indigestible and forbidden.

Simple Reasons

When confronted with the why
of my Saturday mornings
carved from the breast meat
of my frantic, frenetic days,

I smile to myself and know
that all the simple reasons stated
sound foolish
but he has chosen the foolish, hasn't he?

Who, in the faded jaded world
would believe that the simple reason
is the simple pleasure of serving,
and seeing, and smelling
the familiar, changing scene.

How could I trade that first hour
washed with riches music sung
by a voice of velvet opulence wrapped
in sea shanties and love songs
and if I'm lucky, that most wonderful
of laughs?

Then hours of chat and change and exchange
comment and commotion
joy and sorrow and friendship
are not to be traded for the seduction of
an extra hour
of sleep
or anything
another incarnation of Saturday morning
might have otherwise granted me.
(March 1997)

Control

What control do I own here
with days spread before me like
a crazy quilt, herringboned together
with tracks of predictable, plodding stitches?

The year should feel as fresh
as the biting wind atop this hill where I live.
Yet gnawing uncertainty ferrets its teeth through
the place where peace should rest.

Grasping, greedy,
seeking joy as though it were
a thing to be bought,
if only I had enough coin to scrape
into a shining heap?

Searching for shards of my shattered dreams?
Madness!
I demand the restored original!
I will know the whole
when I find it again.
It is in here,
somewhere.

Chain Reaction

My mind was focused through my gloved hands
on the steering wheel
distracted by the 8:35 sports scores on CBC
speeding two and a half klicks from home –

I beetled through the yield sign
cornering the musical slush,
ahead of the lumbering beer truck,
ahead of the impatient green pickup –
I whipped triumphantly toward my destination,
the tiny fishtail wiggle only augmenting
the thrill of timely arrival.

Suddenly –
the sun, through translucent cloud cover
glowed in throbbing quicksilver
above Citadel Hill –
this epiphany of beauty sliced through the
Monday morning workday automation.

Only then, I noticed the splash of colour
that the red-barked dogwood makes
against the stark white cover of the Commons

Only then, was I aware of the lilting step of a
smiling, oblivious schoolgirl lost in a private dream
but betrayed by her body's joy

Only then, did I notice the willow tree, struggling to grow
where humans once hung to die
in public humiliation
Their horror reverberated through my mind
in the minute it took
for the light to change from red to green.

Hunter of Lies

I should like to make incidental note
of the distinct lack of fervour
in your voice
as you declared your undying love –
Tired tones barely crept from
your constricted throat
and I heard a sigh
I'm sure I heard a sigh!

Words that did not match the mating
of sound, and force
struck my ear with wrenching dissonance –
The truth was more in the passage of air
from your throat
than in the syllables forced through
your lying lips.

You are betrayed,
unskilled in duplicity
revealed by mere air
You are betrayed to me.

I am the hunter of lies.
The trails of our shifting eyes and
back leaning body
reveal the hiding places of truth

I am the hunter of lies –
Although bound by the temporal parameters of
my eyes and ears
my skin tingles with the knowing
of when words and body betray.

Right

Have I a right
to such delight
and delicious anticipation
as Divine Comedy is written
before my eyes
and irony, sweet irony
celestial irony
plays out before my sight?

The Wind on Needham Hill

Alone and on the edge of sleep
I live with the furious howling wind
atop this hill,
howling as though the sorrow
and fear of all the world
were unleashed on this
little insignificant drumlin
on the edge of the ocean.

My old house shudders
beneath my feet
the deep bass rumble of rushing air
abuses the corners where the cats
take refuge on calmer nights.

I am certain every loose trash can
has found its way
to the nether world of windswept debris.

I know for certain
wind and rain over frozen ground
will equal water
in my cellar –

Never mind.
The scent of musty basements is
a time warp for me,
taking me back to
interesting times.

I know some science man,
somewhere,
can give me physical laws for why
and when the wind comes,
but it mocks the knowing
and still sends deep primordial
panic racing through
the stem of my brain, here,
half asleep.

The Final Word

In the deep of the night I am weary
and yet my muse is battering down my door
and I cannot refuse her.

I let her enter.
These words pour from my fingers as though
time and temporality were figments or fragments
of my imagination, and utterly
irrelevant.

She is possessing me.
The possession is a far more pleasant thing
than the barrenness.
Chastened by thoughts of bed I allow my fingers to wander
over the letters.

Thousands upon thousands of thoughts
are flickering in their paths.
Tulips in the snow, the first daffodil
and inexorable evidence of spring
leaps from the muck of winter.
Thank you. (What will this summer bring?)
How will I survive another disappointment?
Where are the fresh linens I hung out yesterday?
Base and pure, profound and petty, all scuffle for first place.

Thoughts of the women I love in my life.
Past, present and future clashing,
a torrent of emotion and joy.
Friends as dear as sisters never known.
The Spirit resonates in my being
for the pain felt, the trials endured, the despair voiced.

Please let thy kingdom come,
thy will be done on earth as it is in heaven.

I am tired, yet the Presence is now beyond simply feeling
and is beyond my mere mortality.
The Presence is within, embracing, reminding, loving,
chastening, rejoicing, encouraging.

What a wondrous, precious, awesome, freeing,
deep and abiding Presence! What a gift.
The Presence is sustaining my spirit at all times.
I drop deep within myself to worship and praise,
and living waters rush out to meet my thoughts,
overflowing to thundering cataracts of joy.

The words scribed long ago leap from the page
to speak directly to me,
testifying to the Presence within.
The testimony of long dead brethren
resonates truth within my soul.

Why me? Why now?
If the Presence ever withdrew,

I would cease

to exist.